EMMANUEL JOSEPH

Eco-Psyche, The Intersection of Mental Health, Nature, and Creative Vision

Contents

1

Chapter 1: Awakening the Mind

In a world inundated with noise and relentless hustle, the sanctuary of nature provides a haven for mental clarity and rejuvenation. Every so often, city dwellers seek solace in the wilderness, yearning for a connection that calms the turbulent mind. Take, for example, Sarah, a high-powered executive who finds herself overwhelmed by the unending demands of her job. A weekend in the mountains, surrounded by towering trees and the soothing rush of a nearby river, transforms her stress into tranquility. As she hikes along the trails, Sarah experiences a profound awakening that recharges her spirit and sharpens her mental acuity, illustrating the potent therapeutic effects of nature on the mind.

Sarah's first day in the mountains begins with a sense of unease, her mind still tethered to the office. However, as she takes her first steps onto the trail, the cacophony of the city fades into the background. The rustling leaves and chirping birds replace the incessant ringing of her phone. With each breath of crisp, clean air, Sarah feels the weight on her shoulders begin to lift. The physical act of walking, coupled with the serene surroundings, acts as a natural balm for her frazzled nerves.

As Sarah delves deeper into the forest, she encounters a small clearing bathed in sunlight. She decides to rest here, taking a moment to absorb the beauty around her. The vibrant colors of wildflowers, the gentle hum of insects, and the distant murmur of the river create a symphony that soothes her soul. In this moment of stillness, Sarah feels a connection to the natural world that she had forgotten in her bustling city life. Her mind begins to quiet, and a sense of peace settles over her.

As the weekend progresses, Sarah's immersion in nature continues to work its magic. She finds herself waking up with the sun, her body attuned to the natural rhythms of the environment. Her mornings are spent exploring the diverse landscapes of the mountains, each new sight a reminder of the beauty and wonder of the world. By the end of her retreat, Sarah feels revitalized, her mind clearer and her spirit lighter. The experience serves as a powerful reminder of the importance of reconnecting with nature for mental well-being.

2

Chapter 2: The Healing Power of Green Spaces

Urban environments can feel suffocating, with their concrete expanses and the cacophony of urban life. However, the presence of green spaces within cities offers a breath of fresh air, quite literally and metaphorically. John, a university student grappling with anxiety, discovers a hidden gem—a small, lush park nestled between towering buildings. Spending his afternoons there, he notices his stress levels decrease and his ability to focus improve. The greenery envelops him, acting as a natural balm that soothes his troubled psyche. John's story exemplifies how accessible green spaces can play a vital role in fostering mental well-being amidst urban chaos.

John's daily routine is a relentless cycle of lectures, assignments, and social obligations, leaving him with little time to unwind. The constant pressure takes a toll on his mental health, and he begins to experience frequent bouts of anxiety. One day, while exploring the city, he stumbles upon a small park that he had never noticed before. The park is a verdant oasis, filled with towering trees, colorful flowers, and winding paths.

Intrigued, John decides to take a break from his hectic schedule and spend some time in the park. As he finds a quiet spot to sit, he feels a sense of calm wash over him. The sights and sounds of nature have a soothing effect, and he begins to relax for the first time in weeks. Over the following days, John makes it a habit to visit the park regularly. He finds that these moments of respite amidst nature help him manage his anxiety and improve his overall mood.

The park becomes John's sanctuary, a place where he can escape the pressures of university life and find solace in the beauty of the natural world. As he spends more time in the park, he begins to notice subtle changes in his well-being. His concentration improves, his stress levels decrease, and he feels more optimistic about the future. The experience reinforces the importance of green spaces in urban areas and their role in supporting mental health.

3

Chapter 3: Nature's Prescription for Creativity

Artists and creators often seek inspiration in the natural world, where the beauty and complexity of landscapes ignite the creative spark. Clara, a painter struggling with a creative block, embarks on a journey through the countryside. She sets up her easel by a serene lake, where the vibrant colors of the flora and the gentle ripples of the water become her muse. Each brushstroke becomes a reflection of the natural wonders before her, rekindling her artistic vision. Clara's experience highlights how nature can serve as a boundless source of creativity, enabling individuals to tap into their artistic potential with renewed vigor.

Clara had always found inspiration in the world around her, but lately, her creativity had hit a wall. No matter how hard she tried, she couldn't seem to capture the essence of her subjects on canvas. Frustrated and disheartened, she decides to take a break from her studio and venture into the countryside in search of new inspiration. She hopes that the change of scenery will help reignite her artistic passion.

Upon arriving at a picturesque lake, Clara is immediately struck by the beauty of the surroundings. The water's surface shimmers in the sunlight, reflecting the vibrant hues of the surrounding flora. She sets up her easel and begins to paint, allowing the natural beauty to guide her brushstrokes. As she works, she feels a renewed sense of creativity and purpose. The colors and shapes of the landscape flow effortlessly onto her canvas, and she realizes that her artistic vision has been revitalized.

Clara's experience by the lake serves as a reminder of the powerful connection between nature and creativity. By immersing herself in the natural world, she is able to tap into a wellspring of inspiration that had eluded her in the confines of her studio. The experience not only rekindles her artistic passion but also reinforces the importance of seeking out nature as a source of creative inspiration.

4

Chapter 4: Forest Bathing and Its Benefits

The Japanese practice of "forest bathing" or Shinrin-yoku emphasizes immersing oneself in the forest atmosphere to enhance physical and mental health. Marcus, a tech-savvy entrepreneur, frequently escapes to the dense forests outside the city to engage in this practice. As he walks mindfully among the trees, his senses come alive—the scent of pine, the rustle of leaves, and the dappled sunlight filtering through the canopy. This mindful connection with nature reduces his stress and improves his overall well-being, illustrating the profound benefits of forest bathing in today's fast-paced world.

Marcus is constantly connected to his devices, juggling multiple projects and responsibilities. The constant influx of information and the demands of his work leave him feeling overwhelmed and drained. Seeking a way to recharge and find balance, he learns about the practice of forest bathing and decides to give it a try. He hopes that spending time in nature will help him disconnect from the digital world and reconnect with himself.

On his first forest bathing excursion, Marcus is struck by the tranquility of the forest. The scent of pine needles fills the air, and the gentle rustle of leaves creates a soothing symphony. As he walks mindfully among the trees, he begins to feel a sense of calm wash over him. The sights, sounds, and smells of the forest engage his senses, drawing his focus away from his worries and into the present moment.

As Marcus continues to practice forest bathing, he notices significant improvements in his well-being. His stress levels decrease, his sleep quality improves, and he feels more energized and focused. The experience reinforces the importance of taking time to immerse oneself in nature and the profound benefits it can have on mental and physical health. Through forest bathing, Marcus finds a much-needed respite from the demands of modern life and a deeper connection to the natural world.

5

Chapter 5: Reconnecting with Roots

Modern life often leads individuals to disconnect from their ancestral ties and cultural heritage. However, nature serves as a bridge that reconnects them with their roots. Maria, a second-generation immigrant, feels a deep longing to understand her family's history. She visits the countryside where her grandparents once lived, immersing herself in the landscapes that shaped their lives. Through this journey, Maria gains a deeper appreciation for her heritage and finds a sense of belonging. Her story underscores the importance of nature in fostering a connection to one's cultural identity and history.

Maria had always felt a disconnect from her family's heritage, having grown up in a different country with different customs. Her grandparents often spoke of their homeland with fondness, describing the rolling hills, fertile fields, and vibrant forests. Determined to understand her roots, Maria decides to visit the countryside where her grandparents once lived. She hopes that by immersing herself in the landscapes that shaped their lives, she will gain a deeper connection to her heritage.

As Maria explores the countryside, she is struck by the beauty and serenity of the landscapes. The rolling hills stretch out before her, dotted with wildflowers and grazing livestock. She visits the small village where her grandparents grew up, and the stories they had shared with her come to life. The experience is both nostalgic and enlightening, as Maria gains a newfound appreciation for her family's history and the land that shaped their identity.

Through her journey, Maria finds a sense of belonging that she had longed for. The natural world serves as a bridge, connecting her to her roots and helping her understand her place in the world. Her story highlights the importance of nature in fostering a connection to one's cultural heritage and the profound impact it can have on an individual's sense of identity and belonging.

6

Chapter 6: Nature as a Therapist

Nature has the remarkable ability to act as a silent therapist, offering solace and support during times of emotional turmoil. After experiencing a significant loss, James finds it difficult to navigate his grief. He retreats to a secluded beach, where the rhythmic waves and the vast expanse of the ocean provide a comforting backdrop for his healing journey. The natural environment becomes a safe space where he can process his emotions and find peace. James's experience demonstrates how nature's presence can offer therapeutic benefits, helping individuals cope with and overcome personal challenges.

James had always found comfort in the familiarity of his routines, but the sudden loss of a loved one left him feeling adrift. Seeking solace, he decides to spend a few days at a secluded beach he had visited as a child. The rhythmic sound of the waves crashing against the shore and the expansive view of the horizon create a sense of calm that he hadn't felt in months. As he walks along the beach, collecting shells and watching the seabirds, James begins to feel a glimmer of hope.

The beach becomes James's sanctuary, a place where he can confront his grief without judgment or distraction. He finds comfort in the natural rhythms of the ocean, which seem to mirror the ebb and flow of his emotions. The vastness of the sea helps him put his loss into perspective, reminding him that life continues despite his pain. Over time, James learns to find peace in the natural world, allowing it to guide him through his healing journey.

Through his experience, James discovers the therapeutic power of nature. The beach provides a space for him to process his emotions, find solace, and begin to heal. His story highlights the importance of connecting with the natural world during times of emotional turmoil and the profound impact it can have on mental health and well-being.

7

Chapter 7: The Power of Silence

In a world filled with constant noise and distractions, the silence of nature offers a rare opportunity for introspection and self-discovery. Emily, an overworked journalist, takes a solo trip to a remote cabin in the woods. The absence of modern amenities and the enveloping quietude allow her to reconnect with her inner thoughts and aspirations. The stillness of the forest becomes a canvas for self-reflection, helping Emily gain clarity and direction in her life. Her story highlights the transformative power of silence in fostering personal growth and mental clarity.

Emily's life is a whirlwind of deadlines, interviews, and constant communication. The relentless pace leaves her feeling drained and disconnected from her own needs and desires. Desperate for a break, she decides to rent a remote cabin in the woods for a week. The cabin is surrounded by dense forest, with no Wi-Fi or cell service, providing the perfect environment for her to unplug and unwind.

At first, the silence feels unfamiliar and even unsettling. Emily is used to the constant buzz of the city and the background noise of her devices. But as she spends more time in the quietude of the forest, she begins to appreciate the stillness. The absence of distractions allows her to focus on her thoughts and emotions, providing a space for introspection and self-discovery. She spends her days hiking, journaling, and simply sitting by the fireplace, listening to the sounds of nature.

By the end of her retreat, Emily feels a renewed sense of clarity and purpose. The silence of the forest has allowed her to reconnect with her inner self and gain a deeper understanding of her aspirations. Her experience underscores the importance of finding moments of silence in our noisy world and the transformative power it can have on personal growth and mental well-being.

8

Chapter 8: Nature's Role in Community Building

Nature has the power to bring people together, fostering a sense of community and shared purpose. In a small town, residents come together to create a community garden, transforming a neglected lot into a vibrant space of collaboration and growth. Neighbors of all ages contribute their skills and knowledge, building strong bonds and a sense of belonging. This communal project not only beautifies the area but also strengthens the social fabric of the town. The story of this community garden illustrates how nature can serve as a catalyst for community building and collective well-being.

The small town had seen better days, with many residents feeling disconnected and disheartened. However, a group of passionate individuals decided to take matters into their own hands. They identified a neglected lot in the center of town and envisioned it as a thriving community garden. With a shared vision and a commitment to revitalizing their town, they set to work transforming the space.

As the garden took shape, more and more residents joined the effort. Children planted seeds, seniors shared their gardening wisdom, and families spent weekends working side by side. The garden became a hub of activity and connection, where neighbors could collaborate, learn, and grow together.

The act of tending to the garden fostered a sense of pride and ownership in the community, as well as a deeper connection to the natural world.

The community garden not only beautified the town but also strengthened the social fabric. It became a place where people of all ages and backgrounds could come together, share their knowledge, and build lasting relationships. The story of this garden highlights the role of nature in fostering a sense of community and the positive impact it can have on collective well-being.

9

Chapter 9: The Therapeutic Garden

Therapeutic gardens are designed to promote healing and well-being, offering a serene environment for patients and caregivers alike. In a hospital setting, a carefully curated garden provides a peaceful retreat for patients undergoing treatment. Sarah, a nurse, witnesses firsthand how spending time in the garden helps patients manage their anxiety and improve their mood. The combination of sensory experiences—the sight of blooming flowers, the sound of trickling water, and the touch of soft grass—creates a therapeutic atmosphere that supports recovery. This chapter explores the significant impact of therapeutic gardens on mental health and healing.

Sarah had always believed in the healing power of nature, but it wasn't until she started working at a hospital with a therapeutic garden that she truly witnessed its impact. The garden was a meticulously designed space, with winding paths, vibrant flowers, and soothing water features. It provided a serene escape for patients and caregivers, offering a moment of respite from the sterile hospital environment.

Sarah observed how patients' faces would light up when they entered the garden. The sensory experiences—the sight of colorful blooms, the sound of trickling water, and the touch of soft grass—created a calming and uplifting atmosphere. Patients who spent time in the garden reported reduced anxiety, improved mood, and a greater sense of well-being. The garden became a vital part of their healing journey, providing a space where they could relax, reflect, and connect with nature.

The therapeutic garden also benefited caregivers, offering them a peaceful retreat where they could recharge and find solace. Sarah herself found comfort in the garden, using her breaks to take a moment of mindfulness amidst the greenery. The experience reinforced her belief in the importance of incorporating nature into healthcare settings and the profound impact it can have on mental health and healing.

10

Chapter 10: Nature-Inspired Meditation

Meditation practices inspired by nature can enhance mindfulness and emotional balance. David, a corporate manager, incorporates elements of the natural world into his meditation routine. He visualizes himself walking through a tranquil forest, feeling the cool breeze and hearing the gentle rustle of leaves. This nature-inspired meditation helps him stay grounded and centered, reducing stress and increasing his overall well-being. David's story showcases how integrating nature into meditation practices can deepen the experience and provide lasting mental health benefits.

David's job as a corporate manager was demanding, with long hours and high-pressure deadlines. He often found himself feeling stressed and overwhelmed, struggling to find a sense of balance. Seeking a way to manage his stress, he decided to incorporate meditation into his daily routine. However, he found it difficult to quiet his mind and stay focused during his sessions.

One day, David stumbled upon a guided meditation that incorporated elements of nature. As he followed along, he visualized himself walking through a tranquil forest, feeling the cool breeze on his skin and hearing the gentle rustle of leaves. The imagery transported him to a peaceful place, allowing him to fully immerse himself in the meditation. He felt his stress melt away, replaced by a sense of calm and centeredness.

Inspired by this experience, David began to incorporate nature-inspired imagery into his regular meditation practice. He would visualize himself by a serene lake, on a mountaintop, or walking through a meadow. These nature-inspired meditations helped him stay grounded and connected, reducing his stress and improving his overall well-being. David's story highlights the powerful connection between nature and mindfulness, and how integrating natural elements into meditation can enhance the experience and provide lasting mental health benefits.

11

Chapter 11: Adventures in the Wild

Adventurous pursuits in nature offer a unique way to boost mental resilience and personal growth. Lisa, an avid hiker, embarks on a challenging trek through a rugged mountain range. The physical exertion and the awe-inspiring landscapes push her to her limits, teaching her valuable lessons in perseverance and self-reliance. The thrill of adventure and the beauty of the natural world combine to create an unforgettable experience that enhances her mental strength. Lisa's journey exemplifies how adventurous activities in nature can foster personal growth and resilience.

Lisa had always been drawn to the outdoors, finding joy in exploring new trails and experiencing the beauty of nature. However, she felt a growing desire to challenge herself and push beyond her comfort zone. She decided to embark on a solo trek through a rugged mountain range, a journey that would test her physical and mental limits.

The trek was demanding, with steep climbs, unpredictable weather, and long days on the trail. But with each step, Lisa felt a sense of accomplishment and resilience. The awe-inspiring landscapes, from snow-capped peaks to lush valleys, provided a constant source of motivation and wonder. The physical exertion and the challenges she faced along the way taught her valuable lessons in perseverance and self-reliance.

12

Chapter 11: Adventures in the Wild

Lisa's adventure in the wild not only strengthened her body but also fortified her mind. Each day presented new challenges, from navigating rocky terrain to braving sudden storms. Through it all, Lisa discovered an inner resilience she hadn't known she possessed. The solitude of the mountains provided ample time for reflection, and the sheer majesty of the landscapes instilled a sense of awe and gratitude. By the end of her trek, Lisa emerged not only physically stronger but also mentally rejuvenated. Her journey exemplifies how adventurous activities in nature can foster personal growth and resilience, offering valuable lessons that extend far beyond the trails.

13

Chapter 12: Embracing Eco-Psyche

The concept of Eco-Psyche emphasizes the interconnectedness of mental health, nature, and creative vision. By embracing this holistic approach, individuals can cultivate a deeper sense of well-being and purpose. Jane, a writer and environmental advocate, integrates Eco-Psyche principles into her daily life. She spends time in nature, practices mindfulness, and draws inspiration from the natural world for her creative endeavors. Through this balanced approach, Jane finds fulfillment and a profound connection to the environment. Her story serves as a testament to the transformative power of Eco-Psyche in enhancing mental health and creative expression.

Jane's journey begins with a deep-seated desire to live in harmony with nature. She recognizes that her mental health and creativity are intricately linked to the natural world. To embrace the principles of Eco-Psyche, Jane makes a conscious effort to spend time outdoors each day. Whether it's a walk through a nearby forest, a visit to a botanical garden, or simply sitting by a river, these moments in nature become a cornerstone of her daily routine.

Mindfulness practices, such as meditation and deep breathing, help Jane stay grounded and centered. She incorporates elements of nature into her mindfulness exercises, visualizing herself in serene natural settings and drawing on the sensory experiences of the outdoors. This connection to nature enhances her sense of inner peace and emotional balance, allowing her to approach life with a calm and clear mind.

In her creative work, Jane finds endless inspiration in the natural world. Her writing reflects the beauty and complexity of the environments she explores, and her advocacy efforts focus on preserving these precious landscapes for future generations. By embracing Eco-Psyche, Jane discovers a profound sense of purpose and fulfillment, knowing that she is contributing to the well-being of both herself and the planet.

Through the stories of Sarah, John, Clara, Marcus, Maria, James, Emily, the community gardeners, the hospital patients, David, Lisa, and Jane, "Eco-Psyche: The Intersection of Mental Health, Nature, and Creative Vision" illustrates the transformative power of nature in enhancing mental health and fostering creative expression. The book serves as a reminder of the profound connections between our minds, our environments, and our creative potential, encouraging readers to explore and embrace the healing and inspiring power of the natural world.

Eco-Psyche: The Intersection of Mental Health, Nature, and Creative Vision

In the midst of modern life's chaos, "Eco-Psyche" unearths the profound connection between mental health, nature, and creative expression. This engaging book explores how immersing oneself in natural environments can rejuvenate the mind, ignite creativity, and foster a deep sense of well-being.

Through a series of captivating stories and thought-provoking reflections, readers are introduced to individuals from various walks of life who find solace, inspiration, and healing in nature's embrace. From high-powered executives escaping to tranquil mountains, to artists reigniting their creative spark by serene lakes, each chapter reveals the transformative power of the natural world.

Discover the therapeutic benefits of green spaces, the serenity of forest bathing, and the quiet wisdom found in nature's silence. Learn how community gardens can strengthen social bonds, how therapeutic gardens can promote healing, and how adventurous pursuits in the wild can foster resilience.

"Eco-Psyche" invites readers to embrace a holistic approach to mental health and creativity, highlighting the timeless wisdom of the natural world. Through its pages, find inspiration to reconnect with nature, cultivate mindfulness, and unlock your creative potential.